Shelly Hen
lays eggs

KANEPRESS

AN IMPRINT OF ASTRA BOOKS FOR YOUNG READERS

New York

follow
my food

For Matthew—*DC*

For Thomas and Leo—*JG*

Text copyright © 2022 by Deborah Chancellor
Illustrations copyright © 2022 by Julia Groves

First published in the United States in 2024 by Kane Press,
an imprint of Astra Books for Young Readers, a division of Astra Publishing House
astrapublishinghouse.com
Printed in China

Originally published in Great Britain in 2021
by Scallywag Press, London

Library of Congress Cataloging-in-Publication Data
Names: Chancellor, Deborah, author. | Groves, Julia, illustrator.
Title: Shelly Hen lays eggs / by Deborah Chancellor ; illustrated by Julia Groves.
Description: First edition. | New York : Kane Press, an imprint of
Astra Books For Young Readers, [2022] | Series: Follow my food |
Summary: "A child narrator tells the story of Shelly, a free-range hen; she pecks and scratches
for food, roosts with her flock, and lays eggs that the narrator helps the farmer collect.
Backmatter includes a matching game, more information about chickens, other animals
that lay eggs, and a kid-friendly recipe"— Provided by publisher.
Identifiers: LCCN 2023024704 (print) | LCCN 2023024705 (ebook) |
ISBN 9781662670725 (hardcover) | ISBN 9781662670718 (ebk)
Subjects: LCSH: Hens—Juvenile literature. | Chickens—Juvenile literature.
| Eggs—Juvenile literature.
Classification: LCC SF487.5 C43 2022 (print) | LCC SF487.5 (ebook) | DDC
636.5—dc23/eng/20230630
LC record available at https://lccn.loc.gov/2023024704
LC ebook record available at https://lccn.loc.gov/2023024705

First American edition, 2024

10 9 8 7 6 5 4 3 2 1

Design by Ness Wood.
The text is set in Foundry Sans Medium.
The title is hand lettered.
The illustrations are created in cut paper and digital media.

Shelly Hen
lays eggs

by Deborah Chancellor

illustrated by Julia Groves

KANEPRESS

New York

Shelly is a happy and healthy free-range hen. She roams about outside and lays the prettiest eggs.

In the morning, Shelly takes a dust bath
to shake off pesky mites.
It's the best way to keep her
fancy feathers clean.

Then Shelly pecks the ground, searching and scratching for juicy bugs and tasty greens.

Shelly likes to hang out with her flock.

They cluck . . . and peck . . .

and peck . . . and cluck . . .
the whole day long.

Shelly chases her friends up and down the ramp.
They all know she's the one in charge.

Fussing and flapping makes Shelly feel sleepy.
She finds a shady place to nap . . .

but soon, she will be up and pecking again.

At sunset, Shelly
returns to her safe
and cozy coop.

She roosts in her usual top spot, resting her head beneath her wing.

As the new day dawns, the hens shuffle to their nesting boxes.

Shelly settles down next to her friend
and lays a beautiful brown egg.

The farmer brings food
and water for Shelly's flock.
I help to collect all the eggs
they have laid.

I take a carton of eggs home
and eat one for a snack.
It is wonderfully fresh!

Follow the egg trail to match the words and pictures.

A free-range hen can choose to go outdoors to feed and play during the day.

A flock is a big group of the same kind of bird.

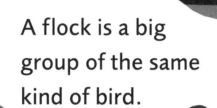

A coop is a hen house that keeps hens warm and safe at night.

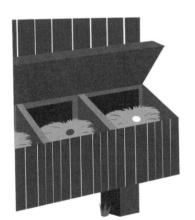

There is a yellow yolk inside every egg. The exact shade of yellow depends on what the hen has been eating.

A nesting box is the part of a coop where a hen goes to lay her eggs.

When a hen perches somewhere to sleep or rest, she is roosting.

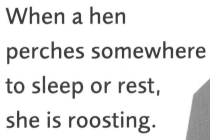

Happy hens

Free-range hens like Shelly live a fun and active life, with plenty of space to run, jump, and play. During the day, they can go outside whenever they want, to feed and take exercise. By night, they roost together in a big coop to stay safe from foxes and other hungry predators. Hens usually lay one egg a day. The older the hen, the bigger the egg!

Tasty eggs

Some kinds of hens lay white eggs, and others lay brown or even blue ones. Whatever the color, eggs are very good for you. Egg whites and yolk contain vitamins, minerals, and protein, which give you energy, help you grow and keep you well. You can also eat the eggs of ducks, geese, ostriches, and emus.

Chatty chickens

Chickens talk to each other all the time, making over twenty-four different kinds of sounds. Each sound means something different, like "I'm feeling comfy," or "Go away!" Hens can live together happily, but always know who's boss. Every flock has a pecking order, and every hen has her own special place in the group.

Eggs to eat

All birds lay eggs — not just chickens. We can eat the eggs
of many different birds. Some eggs are enormous!

quail

chicken

duck

turkey

ostrich

goose

Scramble an egg

Eggs can be cooked in lots of ways, either
by themselves or with other ingredients.
Ask a grown-up to help you make
some delicious scrambled eggs.

You will need:

2 eggs
1 tablespoon of butter
2 tablespoons of milk
Salt and pepper

Instructions:

1. Crack the eggs into a bowl and beat them with a fork.

2. Add the milk to the eggs with a pinch of salt and pepper.

3. Melt the butter in a saucepan.

4. Pour in the egg mixture and keep stirring it with a wooden spoon.

5. When your scrambled egg is cooked, put it on some toast and chow down!

New life

All birds hatch from eggs. Baby chicks can hatch from hens' eggs. For this to happen, a hen must meet a rooster. Then, she sits on her eggs, to keep them warm until they hatch.